Out of Thin Air

Tyler Salomon

BookLeaf
Publishing

India | USA | UK

Presentation by *BookLeaf Publishing*

Web: www.bookleafpub.com

E-mail: info@bookleafpub.com

ISBN: 9789358735192

First edition 2023

ACKNOWLEDGEMENT

To the beautiful people who's helped me get to this point, you have instilled within me great virtues of wisdom and lifelong values, as well as points of perseverance that I will remember to carry with me through this journey. You know exactly who you are, and I can't thank you enough.

Out of Thin Air

Let us commence the story that needs no rabbit
from a hat.
The sole act relies upon the hands that hold a
pen intact.
Like the miracles of cave miners that behold the
world before thee.
Out of Thin Air comes the words from my blood
so lowly.
Out of Thin Air, no one knows where the
formation is from.
They only see the form, but they need to learn
the word, and the letter and emotion embedded
thereof.
Out of Thin Air, like a nuclear football, tis a
recipe for deceit.
If you are a respectful person they will hold your
words against you...you will see.
Because your word is your bond, and by word,
people don't see you.
Your boldest efforts flow forth to bring the
unsung aspects from your very cavern for the
precious nobles to know you.
Precious you thought because your heart you
don't show, so trust is precious like the strands of
a violin bow.

Your heart is not on your sleeve, so easy to
deceive, but the pen can transmogrify the
appearance if in need.
Like the horse hair uncanny and you hold forth
the line, Out of Thin Air your words come for
the occasion in time.
Out of Thin Air can imply coincidental
incidence, but there needs to be an elaborate
definition for this.
Out of Thin Air is not for the quick of heart,
because Out of Thin Air comes the valued
understanding of words and bond from the start.
From value to volume and expansion in width,
the library of singular definition merely begins.
No double talk, or deceit of the sort, but mainly
your time-set strokes on the paper hold forth.
Time being the commodity, and a neuron a
strand, every second is crucial as you bring the
imperative with your heavy hand.
You were meant to bring forth the apocalypse if
need be.
Only God knows what would happen if the
world forgot your tragedy.
No firm court can ever write your wrongs like
you can, so sit down and bring forth the society
to your demand.
Make them understand the power that you
withhold, and bring forth what they made you
force in tenfold.

Foursome and Fourscore, beyond your very
gate, once you understand the power of your
words, placing yourself on the page will live
beyond you as the legacy is written into a perfect
twist and eventual stalemate.

Haiku: Occurrence

Paradoxical.
From vast to ink it becomes
as if it were - none.

The Power of the Nice

There are days when I'm unsure of myself, or of
my decision, therefore notifying the adult is the
best reason.
A reason that's quite simple, yet not often
adhered to, from an age of rare obedience.
I was told my own reasons had no matter due to
my age regardless of reason.
Rather this was a fantasy locked in its place.
Therefore all my fantasies and dreams linked to
the intuition of sheer will abound towards outer
space.
A trap that tied itself as I grew beyond depth,
linking itself to my character of respect.
Now when you walk down the street and see a
person you say is "nice", do not give him your
pearly whites and ask him to assume your
shoeshine.
It shows your ignorance towards niceness and
the knowledge of integrity he/she bears.
Play not on their intelligence because your
assumption of thought will surely rival theirs.
When you yell at such a person for merely
opening their mouth, it shows the gall you
inhabit and your esteem shorter than a stout.

One reason they keep shut or choose to listen
and absorb is because they understand respect
and their place in the world.
No matter how wrong one may choose to be,
albeit a trap, they will search for a way they
wish to achieve...even if there is none.
The first to be picked for a fight.
The first who's open to blame.
The world knows no place for a person hence
you came.
For such a person has not been, or perhaps for a
while, where hope has left aspects deserted, you
brought it with your smile.
They just don't know how to handle it.

No one wants to play with "The Big Red Wagon"

Hello "Everyone" come ho come near!
The Big Red Wagon has come to spread cheer!
Too old and too new, like a can on wheels, but
with my new tricks comes a brand new schpeel!
For every new trick for each girl and each boy,
for children of all ages, I hope you enjoy!

MR. RED WAGON PLEASE GO AWAY!
WE DON'T WANT TO PLAY WITH YOU
TODAY!

Oh don't be so glum, I know you old chum.
I'll stay and keep posting right until you seek
fun.
In all shapes and formats and sizes galore, much
fun in diverse ways, I'll surely find more.

MR. RED WAGON, STOP SINGING TODAY!
I HAVE QUITE A HEADACHE SO PLEASE
GO AWAY!
I JUST WANT TO PLAY PRINCESS BY
MYSELF OKAY?

No problem Suzy, I see you're upset, I can
always talk if you're scared in your own bed.
Perhaps a little candy I can find in my back.
Just hop in the Big Red Wagon and I can help
you find what you ask.

MR. BIG RED WAGON, WE DON'T WANT
NO ADVENTURES TODAY!!
WE ASKED FOR SOME QUIET AND THAT'S
ALL WE ASK FOR OKAY?!
IT'S NOT LIKE WE LEAVE YOU OR WE'RE
CAUSING YOU SORROW, WE JUST DON'T
WANT TO PLAY TODAY, SO WE'LL SEE
YOU TOMORROW!!

Oh...okay. I guess I can see. Well - can I at least
read you a bedtime story?

MR. BIG RED WAGON, IT'S DAYLIGHT
OUTSIDE!!

I'm sorry guys; Wyatt and Suzy.
You won't believe I had another friend say that
to me. I know you guys are pretty busy, so I
won't bother you.

WAIT, WE'RE SORRY MR. RED WAGON!!

That's okay, The Big Red Wagon shall return
another day.
No princess toys, no bats or a ball, do they take
me for a wagon with a gullible stance so tall?
The day we will see, for it is younger than me.
How can I bring meaning to every child I come
across in front of a square screen?
All planted like plants, and happy they seem,
they lose the point of visiting the lands with a
Red Wagon like me.
As I look at the children grow and lose
themselves from me, it breaks my heart, but they
just don't see.
This fun that they have now is very different
from me, seems they have a better friend to
provide all of their needs.
Becoming adventurers and living the dream,
granting them a view that they will surely need.
When they leave their young stouts and expand
with more hair, I wish for them to have that
same memory right there.
With growth, proper discipline, and an
experience quite rare, an adventure abounds
lessons to have their problems ensnared.
With better human beings, comes a better need,
and a much wider lesson to bear fruit indeed.
Alas no need to cry or woefully sway, perhaps
say goodbye to what seems to be this very last
day.

No child, no wife, or anyone else to bare way,
just accept that The Big Red Wagon has no other
friend who wants to play.

Haiku: The Universally Applicable Trope

Princess listens well.
Mirror always loves to tell.
Clueless of herself.

Haiku: A Lesson in Worth

Spaceman now in space.
No contact to bring him back.
What he learned that day.

Haiku: Hammurabi's Cycle

An eye for an eye.
No restraint they continue.
Flaws are embedded.

The Cycle of a Gutless Man

Where blood disintegrates into wind, hinder
transforms into hind, the posterior of a man
continues to find the words to build him.

A voice amidst accountability, where
accountability falls into a trap, that the outside
looking in knows much better than that.

Therefore the accountable person, with selfless
respect for being, will try to learn from what will
be known as a lie from the strangers he's seeing.

Not everyone wishes you well, explaining the
trap of fault, and clinging to more accountability
can suffocate you overall.

This is not your fault, for when you were
growing up, you were told your voice didn't
matter, so what you did was give up.

You put your soul in the elder, the person who
wouldn't betray, but alas for what they shouldn't
commit, they leave the kid running in circles
with a burden that they cannot contest with.

A burden that's not theirs yet they saw all the signs, but tricking an infant to doom is what they're known for through time.

An event that's not even their fault, what a good trap one would say, the unsolved writings and inflicted tears become the burdens you don't know how to escape.

Sins of the father, burdens of the past, they threatened you and told you to take it, with the intention to taunt saying you wouldn't last.

Do not take on the burden of the Gutless Man, the one who was swallowed up inside.

There's at least one within a population trying to endure the cluelessness, guilt, and anger comprised.

Asking for help might not seem like an alternative, but it's the bravest thing. Being alleviated of your weight is more than the ultimate win.

Fear

One ear is sterile, focused, and relieved of all the numbness.
The other ear is contagiously painful, and hollow.
Enters a one-way trip with a deep impact to create a crater so shallow, piling up, bubbling within my veins, therefore making it hard to swallow.
I want to yell, but this description merely downplays the feeling.
My adrenaline is fueled like a gasket when the voice of fear is called.
I seem like a shrimp against a six and a half foot tall embodiment that has enough information about a person to shower them.
It's taller than me.
Fear doesn't exist, but it's the thought of losing everything you cherish.
The action is foreshadowed in the cerebrum.
My action becomes a reality in the cerebellum.
Fear is not real, except when it comes into any physical form possible.
Any form from a centimeter-long bullet to a bulk man that can be quadrupled your size.
Fear is not real, but what you cherish often is.

Fear can put you to the test, so often you question yourself and forget about all the rest.
Fear doesn't rely on facts but more importantly your flaws.
It's a weird emotion, a blend of heart, chaotic commotion, and our darkest nightmares.
This might sound hard but, you have to show fear who's in charge.
Own fear, the task of knowing what's real and what's not.
The struggle of knowing that you can over why the truth says you can't.
The action of defying the truth to create a new one for the rule book.
Whoever you're talking to, what's scaring you, why it's scaring you, but never letting it get the best of you, it's a real struggle.
You are the best you can be.
Fear's facts are so irrelevant that if you listen, it will transform you into a lost, pleading, and soulless incarnate.

The Allusion of what we hate

We are the allusion of the very thing we hate.
People speak on other people and the actions
they take, as they might seem barbaric in nature
give or take.
These actions are quite ravenous, unimaginable
in hate, one would not think of having such a
thing written on their wake.
Sometimes we walk in the patterns in which
we're raised, and from then on within those
patterns, we don't think we could cave.
Be mindful of the situation that one would be in,
there are reasons why people act in the way of
the kin.
Some actions one wouldn't say they condone,
but many things occur when we're sucked into
the unknown.
Just go with an open mind and understand why,
it's a maze of thorns and mallets that rain down
on you in life.
Whether from birth or out of insecurity, it's a
shield they've created, just remember why we
are the allusion of the very thing we hate.

The Most Beautiful Events

The most beautiful events to ever exist are the
ones that you don't think about to begin with.
To think of the atoms as the starting base, you
would think the foundation can continue to
trace.
I recommend you don't just remain in one state,
because there, your thoughts will remain and
await.
Deeper than you and I, don't sleep in the small
town, it tracks you from here to sender and pulls
you down.

The most beautiful events to ever exist are
hidden behind the confines of history.
Most are destined to repeat it because albeit they
bring glory, the greatest achievements are hidden
behind the confines of overrated stories.
Some of the slave masters are given meaning
since they're on the currency, while the others
are given monuments although they make up
half of the story.
The Immortal Tardigrades exist everywhere,
even in the vacuum of space.

A woman gave birth to immortal cells, which later cured many in the medical studies they still take.
Although some of these stories are tragedies, they give birth to bright accomplishments in the human race.

The most beautiful events to ever exist are the ones that require survival of choice.
While your mother was annoyed with you playing in dirt, the Mudskipper rolls within it to keep cool like wearing a shirt.
Its eyes perched seeking out friend or foe, but mainly tries to seek a mate by jumping the highest so all Mudskippers will know.
As you now know of the fish that breathes air and traverses on land, now imagine a bat-like creature of five feet with up to a five-foot wingspan.

The most beautiful events are the ones that are out of touch.
It's not every day you think about a star dying to become a white dwarf too much.
Although we do think about the perils of space, we've rarely thought about the gargantuan creatures beneath your feet in the first place.
Although it's five digits below normal water level and dimension, strong enough for your

lungs to the point of compression, you'll see an
encapsulation of black, but you can't go home,
because you've already passed the aphotic zone.
Just when you thought you couldn't sleep alone
at night, imagine a mere pupil, seemingly the
size of a black hole, opening up its lid right in
front of you that's forty feet high.

The most beautiful events to ever exist are the
ones you know nothing about.
I'm glad you stayed this long as you wish to find
out, what these events may possibly be as you sit
and ponder on your couch.
I suppose I've already taken up much of your
time, so this just might be the end of the line.
Either way, I think it's time for you to go ahead,
use your own two feet, and find more great
events!
With this knowledge comes an opening for a life
you won't wait to spend!
It's easy to think you know everything when you
stay in your own house.
To be honest, ignorance is a fate most people
know nothing about.

Haiku: The Procrastination of Thought

A thought to wonder
about learning everything
wastes time in itself.

Emerson King of Thwaites

Emerson, Emerson, King of Thwaites
Never occurred he'd be the frontrunner at
Kingdom's Gate.
Alloy to the dagger that pierces him awaits.
Ten thousand Destriers stand guard behind the
gravity of his cape.

On the main course is his Kingdom to conquer.
Far and Wide claims that solitude has raised a
hard knocker.
Come one come all for they thought the King
was dead.
The King was awaiting the time of such an end.

Ruination awaits as he charges forth and
straight.
He ponders on the number that will lie in his
wake.
How the folly of quantity can befall one's brain.
All while thunderous crystals slam on the
ground from the cloud of bane.

Last but not least until the King himself
proclaims.

One leg means nothing when a victory so
insatiable is what you crave.
Fall means nothing when you can still crawl to
the gates that arise and you proclaim yourself to
them all.
Inevitable is the rise of the Kingdom of
Thwaites.
He already hears the chants and chivalrous
praise.
Not every enemy relies on the front line.
Enter the fate of the alloy that's revealed from
none other than by the vision of time.

Out of Sight, Out of Mind

Without a Trace
Out of Sight, Out of Mind.
A ghost in the machine.
It remains to be seen.
Such a tool should not be used to simplify ALL
human movement.
Such a weapon should be restricted to simplify
human time and rather be stationed for
improvement in selectable sections.
Humans should still be able to use their minds
and remember the tiresome search and
innovation for it.
What will happen to human innovation?
What will happen to the accomplishments before
that?
What will happen to "the reward?"
What will happen when money is the forefront
of risking one's soul for an entity on the brink of
realizing its inevitable existence within a larger
puzzle piece?
What will happen when the generation after
alpha becomes generation omega and curses our
names upon it?
A selfishly inflicted future all in the name of -
what?

Only because the pressures of business on the forefront and the allocated money needed to be used for it.
If not for the money at stake, there would be no pressures to advance such a thing.
So -
This is where humanity has come to die.
A self induced genocide.
A conscientious decision.
But who cares about anyone else when the vast pleasures are the product given?
Regardless of arguments or suspected treason, what you feed is what's received, and what's received will be released.
A common sense reason for a nonsensical aspect.
When you feed a monkey a drug, it will become rabid.
So why are you shocked when you see its abnormal thirst for blood?

Just some Food for Thought.

Some of the greatest works of art are the ones
that never saw the light of day.
Some of the most successful people have never
gone to college.
Some of the greatest historical figures are the
ones you've never learned in school.
Some of the most scarred human beings are the
ones you never suspect.

If all the greatest technological advances exist as
of now, why is there no cure for cancer?
The talent we've been given for the science we
study is a unique ability.
You pull it straight out of a black hole and study
it attentively.
Recently, a woman born without a uterus was
given a uterus for a baby.
As generic as this sounds this tangibility is not to
be taken lightly.
If confirmed to repair a face or give movement
to stimuli that's incapable of holding its own,
then why has the cure for cancer never been
given access to the ones bedridden in their
home?

If all the money existed in the world as it does
for the sake of better innovation, our children
will live to see the stars and be given fantasies of
interracial nations.
Of all the technology that's built and evolved for
greater purposes in time -
Why has technology for the depths of our sea
never crossed anyone's mind?

Don't be alarmed, as I'm sure you aren't, but
thankfully you've been taught,
that this is just merely a hypothesis for the mind.

Just some Food for Thought.

Pandora, Pandora

Pandora, Pandora, is not a Remora, and neither a
leech on your skin.
She wanders her house, yet has never been
ousted, but is a stranger away from her kin.

In solitary she remains, one would never know
as we see her wander around her five-sided
stage.
From the high angle, she's seen dancing alone,
but it's not an ode to currently living alone.
From a time, within a time, and within a time
alone, to revisit a soul as sweet as candy, a time
before she became The Duchess on the Wall,
and she thought the transition was dandy.

In her solitary mind, she's therefore confined to
the last few items she has. The privilege she
grasps as nothing is promised, so she enjoys it
like it's her last.

From the external, it's hard to believe that
control is out of your reach.
With what she has, and the plane she resides, she
still prays in solitary until her numbered days
pass.

As days become weeks, and weeks become
years, and passages into ad infinitum, hope
should cease, yet it's never released for her faith
retains verbatim.

Through this passage of time, with a woman
divine, in a repetitive plane that can turn one
mad, she's down to the core and to her very
respect, clings to fleeting remains of her identity
- forevermore.

Pandora, Pandora: A Force of Nature

Pandora, Pandora, a name I admire, it seems I can't do it enough.
Quite vibrant for a woman, extraordinary human, reminds of how your vibrance is quite moving.
When expectations are high but overzealously awry she pulls you back on track to your height.
A head in the clouds is how the world is aroused, dreams sometimes feel better than the now.

Pandora, Pandora, my regrets lie with her for I can not switch with her being.
I can handle her pain and through it I gain more insight into what Pandora is seeing.
Her woes I will deal and take everything real for her to receive another chance.
Although she would see herself, with me embodied, she would have no choice but to run and start somewhere else.
To endure her pain would be worth the rain that befalls the new future of this woman.

It isn't just enough to let this woman know that
just her name alone makes the world glow.

Pandora, Pandora, every time I see you, I cherish
your name as it should.
You jump on the front lines, a zone demilitarized
just to teach a friend in need.
You jump in the front as if you're not tired, for
eighteen years I've counted.
I'm not worthy of a friend such as yourself, for
sometimes my anger keeps me far from
soundness.
For these fits that I have are not your own but a
force who tugs on our heart.
It spits on respect, cares not about the prospect,
but says "love" blandly with no regret.

Pandora, Pandora, for all the time I've known
you, I've celebrated you on the pedestal quite
high.
For every time I see you, I'm always reminded
of how my job just cannot suffice.
For every time I always pour out my heart, it is
never enough.
Everything that I have to note about you is
written on every star above.
For every star that's laid and matched, from the
newborn to even the dwarfs.

It still seems like it's never enough for you to see
how your being transcends every word.

Pandora, Pandora, a lovely force of nature, why
do you not wear your crown?
Why can't you understand that you've earned
this all around?
Where I would see myself fail in a stage I
wouldn't prevail at a time where I try to carry
myself.
How can she juggle, a bugger and a few bubbles,
without letting them float away?
Even these words I feel are a downplay to how
elated I feel to see your quirky vibrance every
day.
Although you call them flaws as a thing you
cannot see, you are not a lover, as these words
may seem, but you are much more, and broader,
and not even I can grasp how important you are
to me.

Haiku: The Cycle

Tomorrow Becomes
A day of longing until
You can long no more.

Haiku: Knowledge of the Master

No Master entered.
Their claim of visit - past tense.
Knowledge is not there.

Everybody needs a Friend

There's an appreciation that comes with
providing.
Providing a possible insight that can brighten
someone's day.
A possible word from the mouth can perhaps
open the airway.
Of all the sperm that take the great migration to
reach the ovulated egg, the journey can compare
when the specific words directly penetrate the
heart of a babe.

On that note being said, on the topic of love,
when we move forward as a community, don't
look in the wrong places.
Love is an interdimensional element that
exceeds into the fourth realm beyond our faces.
At face value, it's not external, but there is a
least evident value.
There's the love that's been wrought or
misplaced, or forgotten without you. Perhaps
forgiveness that's waiting, or the love that's
never been expressed or is hopeless due to
words being bitten around the bush for hopes to
express.

Since this is merely the start of a journey to
search, we shall find more about the tangibility
of this element when we walk together.

Hearts grow cold and some become light.
Some have become weary from the fight with
life.
Some hearts ignite from unexpected friends,
whether a gap in age or from years on end,
everybody needs a friend.

Everybody meets an end.

Perhaps a value can define those means - like a
wife or a husband.

Take the time to look, and be not bound by age.
There are people with hearts who have been
trapped in a cage.
By the motions of life or the time one was
raised, a friend can be a great reason to put a
smile on one's face.

Haiku: The Cycle Revisited

Tomorrow Becomes
Present for the following
To be longed again.

www.ingramcontent.com/pod-product-compliance
Lightning Source LLC
LaVergne TN
LVHW010830200726
843508LV00012B/2552